FINANCIAL ADVICE THAT DOESN'T SUCK

FINANCIAL ADVICE THAT DOESN'T SUCK

HOW THE FINANCIAL SERVICES INDUSTRY IS SCREWING YOU AND WHAT TO DO ABOUT IT

Steve Larsen, CPA, CFP®

© 2017 Steve Larsen, CPA, CFP®
All rights reserved.
ISBN-13: 9781974052561
ISBN-10: 1974052567
Library of Congress Control Number: 2017911958
CreateSpace Independent Publishing Platform
North Charleston, South Carolina

Contents

CHAPTER 1

INTRODUCTION

Holy shit. They think we do the same thing.

It was a painful realization that day. A nice couple had been in my office two or three times and were trying to decide what to do with their money. Retirement was approaching at light speed, and they had neither a financial plan nor an advisor they could trust. All they knew was they were receiving conflicting advice from friends, coworkers, and the media about how to be smart with their money and needed to figure out what was going on.

As a financial planner, I had guided them through my typical process, helping them create a plan that would allow them to enjoy retirement. This involved three steps: First, an initial meeting to discover what their goals were. Second, additional meetings to present alternative solutions and explain the pros and cons of each. And third, moving into the implementation phase where my firm would take care of the details for them and execute the plan.

Hundreds of clients have decided to do business with me through this financial planning process, and I like to think everyone one of them was happy with my advice and the results. When we sat down for the third meeting, however, I could tell something had changed.

"What do you know about annuities?" they asked.

"I know I make a ton of money if I sell you one," I replied. "Why do you ask?"

"Well," they said, "it turns out our neighbor does retirement planning too, and we met with him last week."

"That sounds like a great idea," I causally lied. "What firm does he work for?"

They proceeded to tell me that he was an independent advisor—which could mean anything but usually means nothing—and specializes in retirement income planning. He could offer them guaranteed income that they would never outlive. They could make money if the market went up but never lose it if it went down.

"Well," I started…

Actual Conversation	Conversation in My Head
Me: That does sound good. The product he is referring to is called an annuity, and it may very well be a great solution for you.	**Me:** Are you kidding me?
	Them: Excuse me?
Them: Yes, that is what we thought. We really don't want to lose any of our investments. An annuity lets us protect our money, and maybe we can make some too!	**Me:** Somebody is trying to sell you a product, and you are calling it "advice"?
	Them: But they had business cards.
Me: Okay, but we are talking about a product before you have a plan. That is like ordering the cabinets for your house before you have a blueprint. Typically, if we can understand what your goals are, selecting the products will be an easy decision.	**Me:** That dude is not a giver of advice; he is a seller of products. Where do you get advice if you need a new car—from the dealership?
	Them: That's funny; this guy used to sell cars too.
Them: We appreciate your work, but this guy says…	**Me:** Of course he did—like any good financial advisor.

What an awakening. I'm a certified public accountant and certified financial planner. I have a master's degree in accounting and fifteen years of experience in this business. I have turned down countless commissions to do the right thing for my clients. Throughout our meetings, I took the time to understand their goals and then develop the most efficient path for them to get there.

This guy has been insurance licensed for five years and used to sell cars. According to these nice people at my conference table, he and I are on the same playing field.

You must be kidding me. They think we do the same thing.

Everyone is incentivized to sell you, not educate you.

Who to Blame

Why does receiving financial advice that is in your best interests seem like the most complicated thing in the world? Do you have any idea who to call, what to ask for, or how to pay for it? If you have an advisor, do you have a clue how they get paid or how much? You don't have to answer because I already know. This information has been hidden from you, and it is only the tip of the iceberg of how your money is being siphoned from your investment accounts.

Who do we blame for this web of deception, lies, and misdirection that the financial services industry has created? How did it start, and how do we fix it? There is plenty of blame to go around, and everybody will get his or her turn. My favorite targets are the media, the government, financial advisors, investment firms, and the creators of financial products, although the list goes on.

These targets will be easy enough, and we will deal with them in due time. If we want to analyze the real cause of this problem, however, we should look a little closer to home. There is one person who has had a chance to do something about this for almost fifteen years now and has done very little to make a difference: me.

Conspiracy of Silence

How do you boil a frog? Stick him in a pot of cold water, and as the temperature rises one degree at a time, he will never notice the incremental change until it is too late. By the time the frog is up to his neck in scalding water, he has monthly payroll to meet and a mortgage to pay. At some point, it's just too late to make a change.

There are millions of Americans out there who wish they would have taken financial advice from a frog instead of what they experienced. The advice they so desperately craved turned out not to be advice at all but rather the result of a system that was rigged to have them purchase a product. The sale of these products provides benefits and profit for somebody; any guesses whether that person is you?

Your dollars are benefiting a chain of people that continues almost endlessly.

And what have the good guys been doing for decades upon decades as this has been going on? We have been staying silent for the most part. Sure, maybe we make a small ruckus in our little corner of the world. We tell our clients how we are different and crank out a glossy brochure implying that we are one of the good guys. After all, aren't you impressed I'm an *independent advisor?*

And maybe we are one of the good guys and gals. We do the right thing for the client all the time, but sometimes the right thing *still* involves receiving a huge commission check. If we are doing the right thing, why turn down money that somebody is going to make? The logic is hard to argue with, and for quite some time, this plan does work.

But like the boiling frog, we lose our ability to judge when we are in too deep. A line has been crossed, but we have no knowledge or recollection of crossing one. I cannot think of a single instance, even after working with hundreds of clients, where I didn't do the right thing. I can recall many circumstances where I chose a solution that was far less profitable to me because I knew it was the right thing for the client. I truly can't recall a single scenario I should apologize for.

There are two problems with this line of thinking, however. The first is that *all* financial advisors feel they are *always* acting in the client's best interest. Some truly mean it. Others have convinced themselves over the years that their integrity has never been stretched to meet their own needs over their client's needs. You know this is bullshit, I know this is bullshit, but how do we tell who is lying and who isn't?

The second problem—and this isn't unique to financial advice—is we feel that we can manage our own conflicts. All financial advisors believe they are fully equipped to decide right from wrong when in fact we are the *least* equipped humans on earth to make this decision. Our egos are way too large to decide we are judge, jury, and executioner of right and wrong.

Even if an advisor can stay objective and manage his conflicts effectively, we still have one additional glaring and obvious problem: how is the consumer supposed to determine which advisors can manage themselves and which ones can't?

Everyone says they are doing the right thing. Who wouldn't say that? We are back to the inmates running the asylum.

Great advice is an opinion. Conflicts of interest are a fact.

Building a financial services practice that truly looks out for the consumer is like developing healthy eating habits. The real discipline begins at the grocery store when you walk past the junk food aisle and straight to the vegetable section. If you can resist the temptation to have bad food around the house, then you aren't going to snack on it all day.

My goal is to help you understand what advisors are doing at the grocery store, not what they do when they are in the kitchen. Once we are in the kitchen, we can make anything look like a gourmet meal. Have you ever watched one of those baking shows? Everybody looks like a genius during step two, which is the preparation. If you only have healthy ingredients, the chef—by chef I mean advisor, stay with me here—is way more likely to produce a healthy meal.

You have no idea the tricks advisors develop over the years to make whatever investment strategies you are currently using look bad and make whatever they are doing look ten times better. This is our world; we can rearrange and shuffle your financial life until you don't know which way is up.

If you still aren't getting the point, let me clear things up. Imagine a wife is looking for an advisor to help her decide how many times per week she should be having sex. She finds a nice, local counselor who offers her a one-hour session for $150 that will dive into the issues surrounding this decision.

"One hundred and fifty dollars!" the husband says. "That is crazy! Why would you pay someone when I will help you make that decision for free?"

"Are you sure you can be objective?" the wife asks.

"Of course I can," he replies. "Besides, she isn't even helping you ask the right questions. You should be asking how many times *per day*."

Yep, we can all manage our own conflicts.

Wall Street is actively screwing you over…and Main Street is holding the camera.

The Myth of Conflict-Free Advice

Conflicts can be managed, but they can't be eliminated. Picture the mechanic who is recommending the work that needs to be done on your car. The same person who is giving you "advice" will also be doing the work and only making money if you follow his or her advice. The only way to manage this encounter would be to bring in a second mechanic to advise you on the first one. That solution is great conflict management but a horrible use of time and money.

Let's look at professionals who like to consider themselves the standard of independence and objectivity—like lawyers and accountants—to see how "conflict free" they are. If they charge you by the hour, they have incentive to work slower and bill more time. If they charge you a flat fee, they have an incentive to cut corners and get the work done sooner. That isn't to suggest that they do, only that conflict exists even among professionals.

But surely conflicts can't exist everywhere, right? Wrong. Even your local nonprofit is going to be in conflict every hour of every day. What if they want to purchase a new office chair for one hundred dollars? That does not seem like an unreasonable expense to me, but they are not spending that one hundred dollars on services to fulfill their mission of helping those in need. How can you justify taking one hundred dollars away from poor kids so you can have increased lumbar support?

Business conflicts are everywhere. Financial conflicts are the best at hiding.

Did you know that the typical advisor selling an annuity today is making around 7 percent in commission? If you invest $100,000 in an annuity product, the agent is making somewhere around $7,000. I understand why you would think that number sounds ridiculous, but it takes a lot of time, money, and overhead to run a financial services business. Seven thousand dollars for a job well done is in the ballpark of what we should be making per client *if* we know what the hell we are doing—a big if.

If you invest $500,000 rather than $100,000 into that same product, the agent makes $35,000 in commission. Now that is ridiculous. Is this really the person you want to be taking advice from? I'm not just picking on insurance agents either; that is about what I would make as well if you purchase an annuity from a financial planner like me. Should you move

$500,000 into an annuity? I can ethically handle that decision, but how can you be sure today isn't the day I act like everybody else? Maybe today is the day I am sick of my old truck and need a couple of extra bucks to be a Beamer Guy.

Consumers are consuming the wrong thing, making it more difficult and more expensive to reach them. You have a gut feeling that the information you are getting isn't quite right, and so you keep searching, analyzing, and postponing a decision until life events make it difficult to wait any longer.

We are stuck in this unvirtuous cycle of substituting product information for advice.

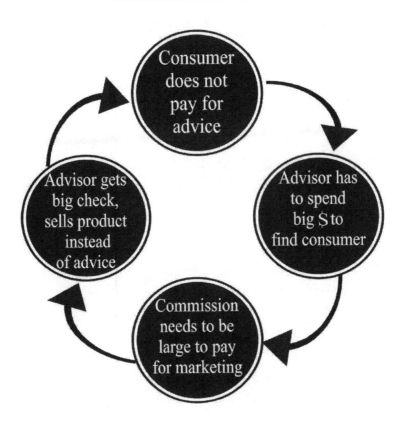

You Can't Get There from Here

We know what the real problem is: there is no system to determine who can give you excellent, unbiased advice. Every financial advisor claims he or she is the only one who can find that magic solution for you, and every investment firm starts to look the same after a while.

Let's be clear though. I am not claiming there is nowhere to *receive* excellent, unbiased financial advice. There are thousands of financial planners in this country who will give you amazing advice for a good value. My point is that no one is providing education on how to find them. The focus is still on "investment education" instead of where it belongs—on "finding a legit advisor to provide that education."

A typical consumer will interview prospective advisors and ask about the performance of their portfolios, or how much their fees are. This is considered proper due diligence on finding an advisor because you don't know what else to ask. When you follow that framework for selecting an advisor, here are the results you get:

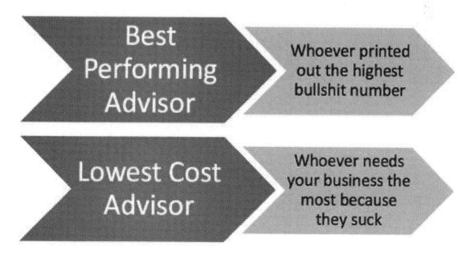

Best Performing Advisor → Whoever printed out the highest bullshit number

Lowest Cost Advisor → Whoever needs your business the most because they suck

It's not your fault you are asking all the wrong questions. There is a billion—trillion?—dollar industry that is dedicated to keeping you confused. After all, if the consumer were informed, the consumer would have to come first. If the consumer came first, this house of cards that Wall Street has built would come tumbling down.

We are not missing great advice and great solutions for the consumer; we are missing a road map for the consumer to find them.

How Did We Get Here?

Like most government initiatives, this one started out with good intentions. The financial markets were loosely regulated until the 1930s, when in the aftermath of the Great Depression, Congress decided to impose new rules on the investment industry. The Securities Acts of 1933 and 1934 addressed how the issuing of investments would be handled. The "issuing" of investments means selling stocks to people.

The Investment Advisors Act of 1940 was later passed to regulate those who were giving investment advice, as opposed to those who were selling stocks. This makes sense: we have one group of people creating and selling products and another group providing advice on whether those products make sense for you. Over the years, however, the two blended together to where the consumer could no longer see the difference.

But the government had our backs, right? Unfortunately, you already know the answer. The original intent of the financial regulations was clear and should not have left a lot of room for interpretation. One group of people would create products to sell, whereas the other group would provide advice and be required to act solely in their clients' best interest. The investment landscape looked like this:

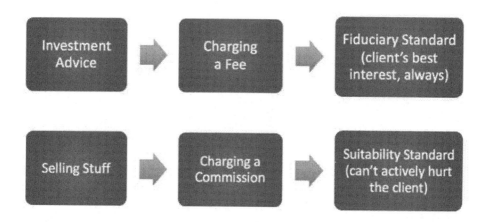

I know this is going to come as a shock, so make sure you are sitting down. (Does anyone read standing up?) A major Wall Street firm influenced our government to its own benefit! I know it's hard to believe, but it happened. Enter the Merrill Lynch rule.

In the late 1990s, the Securities and Exchange Commission (SEC) took a much different interpretation of the law than they previously had. The new interpretation was this: great suggestion, but we will just do what we want.

Now salespeople at Merrill Lynch and other major Wall Street firms could charge a fee for advice and not be subject to the Fiduciary Standard. So now, the investment landscape looked like this:

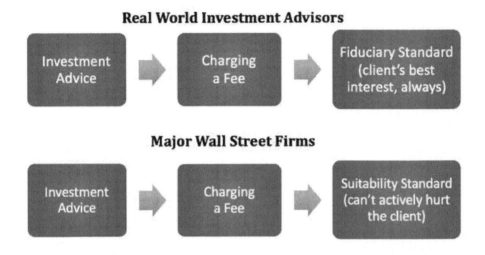

Why does everyone hate Wall Street and think the system is rigged against them? Because it is. This was called the Merrill Lynch rule because there were different sets of standards for different groups of advisors. How does that even happen?

The most disturbing part is that the consumer—you—never even knew this was going on. Everyone reasonably assumed that advisors were subject to the same rules and regulations. Unfortunately, it is not that simple and never has been. Cutting through the layers of lies, misdirection, and skewed incentives will take multiple years and multiple books, but we must start somewhere.

Joe Retirement was busy asking about fees and performance when he should have been asking, "Are you legally obligated to act in my best interest?"

Fiduciary Capital, LLC

Tired of the word *fiduciary* yet? It is in the news a lot these past couple of years, and everyone is trying to figure out what it means. The government thinks a fiduciary rule should mean that you must act in the best interests of your client—unless you don't want to. Just wait—we are only in phase one of making that word mean nothing.

Through the investment license that I hold, my CPA license and my CFP®—for real, the ® is required; I'm not trying to be pretentious—I am required to act as a fiduciary at all times. No matter the circumstances, I must act in the best interests of my client, which sounds reasonable, and I like to think I do. But that doesn't mean I don't have as many conflicts as the next guy.

I may get paid an ongoing fee to manage your portfolio, but if I want to recommend you take money out of your investment account and purchase insurance, I will have a conflict despite my fiduciary status. The insurance product will pay me a commission, but the money will be taken out of the investment account that I am managing for you, so I will make less money on an ongoing basis. Even while I am trying to do the right thing for you, I still must weigh my current revenue versus my future revenue.

Now imagine you are taking money out to purchase insurance through another agent where I won't get paid. Any guesses what my likely recommendation will be?

The good guys *should* be advertising themselves as fiduciaries, but there is more to the story. You need to dig deeper still to understand why you are supposed to use strategy A over strategy B. Strategy A is definitely better for someone. Just be sure that someone is you.

Ten Months in a Year

One of my stops along the way was at a 100 percent independent, fee-only registered investment advisor. We weren't selling commission products and were charging a fee for managing portfolios. Sounds simple enough, right.

One day my partner and I were finishing up a discussion about our updated portfolios, most of which contained ten mutual funds. They were your plain vanilla, very conservative but well-diversified portfolios. They looked good to me, but I noticed some hesitation.

My partner reminded me of our marketing strategy, which was to hold a client event every month. This strategy was working well, and our firm was growing. We had our next several events on the calendar but had not booked out the last couple months of the year.

He reminded me that each of the mutual funds in the portfolio had what we call in the business a "wholesaler," which is basically a salesperson who drops by and convinces us to use his or her products. This person usually drops by the office and takes us to happy hour where we drink decent whiskey and order appetizers, something I certainly don't do on my dime.

The wholesalers provide one other function as well. Once a year they will pay for a decent-size event we put on for our clients. The monthly events we had been holding for our marketing were not coming out of our pocket; the wholesalers of the mutual fund companies we were using in our investment portfolios were paying for them.

Our issue was that we were holding one event every month, twelve per year. Our portfolios contained only ten funds, which meant that we only had ten of our events paid for. Two funds were quickly added to the portfolios to keep our marketing plan on track.

Fiduciary portfolio management at its finest! That style of conducting business is not a fit for me, and I was out of that venture in just over a year. Beware of those who claim fiduciary status the loudest, for there are wolves in sheep's clothing everywhere.

CHAPTER 2

MOTIVES VS. INCENTIVES

I feel like he has my best interests in mind.
—All investors everywhere, based on no evidence, ever

"It's just that it's all so confusing," they said.

"It is so confusing," I replied. "Especially when you are trying to predict the future instead of predicting the present."

More nice people. Most everyone who comes into my office is nice. They have worked hard, saved some money, and just want to make sure they are making good decisions. Whether the clients are old or young, they have this in common: the desire to make a good decision and stick with it.

Like any professional, I enjoy when people show up and listen to my advice. We can move forward and put them on a path to success very quickly, and I happen to think my advice is excellent. But despite my self-proclaimed awesome advice, the route to success is not always a smooth ride.

"We have talked to so many people, and everyone says something different. Why can't anybody agree on what makes sense?" they asked.

"Great question," I said. "Let's run through who is saying what and try to figure it out."

Actual Conversation	Conversation in My Head
Them: Well, we have been reading a lot online, and it says lots of different things. Mostly that advisors charge fees that cost you a lot of money.	**Them:** Well, we have been reading a lot online, and it says lots of different things. Mostly that advisors charge fees that cost you a lot of money.
Me: Yes, most businesses charge for their services. The important thing is to understand what you are paying for.	**Me:** And let me guess, they have a solution for you without charging those "high, unreasonable fees."
Them: And then the guy on the radio says we need to be in 60 percent stocks, 40 percent bonds, and buy term insurance.	**Them:** And then the guy on the radio says we need to be in 60 percent stocks, 40 percent bonds, and buy term insurance.
Me: Okay, how many meetings have you had with him? Does he know anything about your goals and what your risk tolerance is?	**Me:** Yes, generic advice for everyone! Did he have follow-up advice in a book you are supposed to buy?
Them: I guess not. It was just interesting. Then my coworker says we can do it all ourselves online. He is really smart and says he can help me.	**Them:** How did you know that? Anyways, my coworker says we can do it all ourselves online. He is really smart and says he can help me.

Me: He sounds smart. How many people has he helped through retirement? How many financial plans has he done?

Them: None that I know of, but he says it's easy. Then this other advisor says he can provide me with guaranteed income, and we won't have to worry about any of it.

Me: Guaranteed income can definitely play a role in your retirement. Did the guaranteed income product make sense as part of your financial plan?

Them: What financial plan?

Me: Hoo-boy.

Me: I bet he is a freaking engineer. He "solved" investing doing it part time, when PhDs in finance can't do it full time. It's a miracle!

Them: Yeah, he is really smart. Then this other advisor says he can provide me with guaranteed income, and we won't have to worry about any of it.

Me: The product salesman thinks you should buy products—what a shock! Let me take a wild guess: the last surgeon you saw thinks you need surgery?

Them: That guaranteed product seemed like a good financial plan for us.

Me: You must be kidding me.

The great mistake made by consumers is trying to analyze the *motives* of the person who is selling the product instead of his or her *incentives*.

The same things happen over and over in meetings with prospects who are interested in my firm. After a meeting or two where we talk about their goals and I let them know that I have all the answers they will ever need, we start to get down to decision time. Even though we are on the same page financially, one question remains: can I trust him?

For those who do business with me, the answer is yes. But how is someone who does not know me very well supposed to know that? And if everyone wants "an advisor they can trust," how are we supposed to develop a system where a consumer can determine trustworthiness in a matter of days or weeks?

This is difficult to do. The lack of a system for deciding who is honest leads us to scientifically sound statements such as:

- "I went with my gut on this one."
- "I just had a really good feeling about her."
- "He was really genuine and made me feel comfortable."
- "He agrees my grandson Timmy is the best Little League baseball player in the city; he must be a good advisor."

At the end of the day, you are still trying to predict the motives of the person you are meeting with. Does he seem like a good guy or a bad guy? Does she strike me as someone who would screw us over? This is an emotional framework for making decisions because personal finances are very emotional.

Trust should be extended based on facts, not emotion.

Just because finances are emotional to you doesn't mean your decision-making process needs to be. What I tell potential clients who meet with my firm is that you can try to decipher the motives that I and every other advisor in town have until you are blue in the face, but you still won't have a clue when you are done. Instead, you should analyze what our incentives are when we provide advice. By asking *incentive* questions instead of *motive* questions, you will have a better understanding of the present, which will lead to predictable results in the future.

Motive Questions	Advisor Answers
• Can I trust you?	My middle name is trust.
• Will you be there for me when I need you?	I'm here for you 24-7. In fact, I just moved into your spare bedroom.
• Will you act in my best interests?	My Grandpa Joe Fiduciary taught me everything he knows.
Incentive Questions	**Advisor Answers**
• Are you paid more for making one recommendation over another?	?
• Do you have a boss that you report to?	?
• Does your firm have proprietary products it will recommend to me?	?

Financial advisors are easy to pick on. Most of the advisors you will run into in life will be reasonably pleasant, but they also take themselves so seriously it makes all of us easy targets. When I am in a social situation and do not want to make things awkward or end the conversation, I tell the other person I am a CPA. When it's a person I don't want to talk with anymore—or I am trying to skip out of an event early—I tell everyone I am a financial advisor, and I am immediately an outcast.

Does it seem like I am joking? Try telling the next stranger you are introduced to that you are a financial advisor and watch what happens. They immediately close themselves off to you, as if you are going to try and sell them a bottle of snake oil right there on the spot. As an advisor, it's rather amusing to watch this happen, and you get used to it. I need to be honest about my profession and *why* most people react this way.

The standoffish reaction could be for several reasons, but clearly much of the country has not had a good experience with a financial advisor or does not have a good impression of them based on what they have read or heard from others. We have significant hurdles to overcome just to have someone listen to what we are saying with an open mind.

This impression likely begins when a person has an initial meeting with an advisor to determine if they need or want his or her help. The initial meeting typically goes something like this:

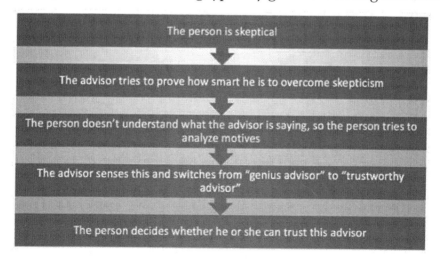

The person is skeptical

The advisor tries to prove how smart he is to overcome skepticism

The person doesn't understand what the advisor is saying, so the person tries to analyze motives

The advisor senses this and switches from "genius advisor" to "trustworthy advisor"

The person decides whether he or she can trust this advisor

And the cycle continues, with another person trying to analyze the motives of a stranger. Nowhere in that dance does the person desperately needing financial advice try to determine whether the advisor has the *incentive* to act in his or her best interests. People continue to "go with their gut" and "trust their instincts" when choosing a relationship that will influence every financial decision they will ever make.

And it doesn't stop with selecting an advisor. Anyone looking for financial advice online or through other media sources will go through a similar process. You may think that by opening yourself up to the catalogs of financial information online, watching CNBC, and turning on AM radio you are finding a more objective source of information.

Unfortunately, you could not be further from the truth. Many of our "financial experts" in the media are burdened with the same conflicts of interest and baggage that everyone else has. Because they are on TV and talk about how you are getting ripped off and how they are "on your side," you get a good feeling about them and want to listen to their advice.

And once again, you are receiving financial advice because you think the source of the information has good intentions, without having any real clue what their incentives are to deliver that advice. If you start digging a little deeper into what is happening behind the scenes, you may be surprised to learn the reasons someone is giving you a recommendation.

It's Not Just Us

As guilty as financial advisors are for creating this mess, we are only part of the problem. The media, Wall Street firms that hire the advisors, and makers of financial products are all to blame for creating mass confusion in the marketplace. How does the saying go—"If you can't dazzle them with brilliance, blind them with bullshit"? If you keep buying things you don't understand, these companies will continue to produce them.

The role of a financial advisor should be to guide you through this mess with as much objectivity and independence as possible. We should have your best interests in mind not because we say we do but because we can prove that we do. With information and misinformation flying at you every day, advisors need to be a resource to help you sort through it all.

When your favorite media personality tells you to implement a certain solution, you assume it is because he or she cares about you, and maybe they do. The reality, however, is that you are giving this person a free pass when analyzing his or her advice—a free pass that you would never give to someone in your own city who you are meeting with in person. Perhaps our standards for receiving advice should apply universally to everyone.

The Media

We are in an interesting period of time where anything a financial advisor may say is guilty until proven innocent and treated with a lot of skepticism. However, when people read a random online article or turn on the radio, any information they receive is assumed to make sense for them until proven otherwise. This isn't right.

Our media resources have conflicts of interest that are just as significant, if not more so, than your neighborhood financial advisor. The advice coming out of the microphone or TV might make sense for us, but do you know what is going on behind the scenes? Everyone is trying to make a buck, and if they can help you, that is just a bonus.

For examples of conflicts in the media, there are two case studies to look at. I have tremendous respect for both men. They have been able to positively impact and influence lives on a scale that I can only dream of.

I don't question the motives of these men. It would be impossible for me to determine what is going on inside of someone's heart and mind. In fact, I would bet my Ken Griffey Jr. rookie cards that they wake up every day with the intention of helping as many people as possible improve their lives. These are men to be admired, not mocked.

But guess what? I wake up every day with the same intention. I just don't have the large audience yet. And we still have our original problem: you will never know if that is our true intention. In fact, you are reading this paragraph starting to wonder about the *motives* of your favorite media personality, when I am trying to teach you to look at the *incentives*.

Dave Ramsey

Through his *Total Money Makeover* book and Financial Peace University, Dave Ramsey has transformed thousands, if not millions, of lives. His primary focus is on helping people develop budgeting habits so they can take control of their finances and get out of debt.

The culture he has built around being smart with your money and focusing on saving is remarkable. As a financial planner, I specifically like how his materials lay out action steps to keep moving forward. The $1,000 emergency fund is a great example of a concrete action that will get someone moving in the right direction.

A quick look on his website confirms that the advice on saving, budgeting, and paying off debt is as great as ever; he is unmatched in this area. The trouble begins where it always does in this business: someone wants a piece of the investment action.

Dave is well known for his Endorsed Local Provider (ELP) program, which will give you a referral to a local Realtor, insurance agent, accountant, or until recently a financial advisor. These ELPs pay a monthly fee to Dave to be the exclusive ELP in his or her area for the particular service.

Several years ago, I had the opportunity to work with a financial advisor ELP in my area, and it was very instructive. Spoiler alert: the system isn't set up to work for the consumer. It was set up to work for one person only and operates according to the outline below.

1. The financial advisor would pay a monthly fee to Dave Ramsey to be part of the ELP program. When I was involved, the number was $350 a month. I heard that number climbed well over $500 in later years.

2. To pay for the marketing costs, the advisor would need to sell products for an up-front commission. If the advisor was not making commissions, they could not afford to pay a large monthly fee to Dave.

3. Dave becomes the only major media personality—that I can find—to recommend buying commission-based mutual funds over options without commissions.

4. The advisor I was involved with would then sell the fresh-eyed Ramsey devotee commission-based investment products as well as life insurance and auto insurance.
5. Commission checks would come in for the advisor, and another year of being an ELP would be purchased.

Rinse and repeat. If you don't think the business model has an influence on the products that are being recommended, I'm not sure what to tell you. I have no cure for naïveté. In fact, for nearly the entire run of the ELP program, Dave Ramsey callers in my area were directed to an advisor who worked for one of the largest insurance companies in the country. These clients were often charged an up-front planning fee just for the privilege of purchasing the companies' own crappy investment products and expensive insurance solutions.

Again, I can't be clear enough that none of this is to question the *motives* Dave has in setting up this system. Tens of thousands of individuals are better off for the system that he put in place. He has improved lives on a scale that I will likely never be able to replicate.

The issue is with the incentives. I would imagine that almost every person who was referred to an ELP thought he or she was receiving independent, objective advice in his or her best interests. They were relying on their perception of his *motives* and not on an understanding of his *business model.*

Recently, the business model has changed for financial advisors associated with Dave Ramsey. Advisors have been removed from the ELP program and are now part of a service called SmartVestor. The reasoning behind this move has not been publicly stated, but I would imagine it deals with the regulations of our business.

"Endorsing" a financial advisor would basically put you on the hook financially for any recommendations that went wrong.

The SmartVestor service will give you names of investment professionals in your area who "put clients first" and "focus on the long term." Advisors must also adhere to the Code of Conduct—because a two-page PDF will ensure integrity!—and the service is free to investors.

If it's free to investors, then who is paying for it? You guessed it: advisors are still paying a monthly fee to be part of the service. You will be sent a list of advisors who need business badly enough to pay Dave Ramsey a monthly fee.

Make no mistake. You will be the one paying for the service at the end of the day. You are submitting your information into an online form to basically get a list of random financial advisors in your area. We continue to trust large companies that give us "free" services. It's quite baffling. Unless you are the one *directly paying* for independent, objective advice, you have a very slim chance of receiving it.

Pay for advice directly, you cheap bastard.

Tony Robbins

I have a confession to make: Tony Robbins has become one of my favorites. I remember a couple of decades ago hearing his name and associating it with cheesy motivational speaking. Of course, I never actually read one of his books or took a course from him; as a young man, I had everything figured out and clearly did not need help from anybody. That illusion was a lot of fun while it lasted.

In the last several years as he has greatly expanded his media presence, I have consumed some of his books, videos, and event recordings. The directness and speed with which he can positively impact lives is astounding, and it is easy to respect someone who you perceive as nearly everything you are not. The ability to maintain that level of energy and positivity is impressive. I must have missed the day in CPA school where they taught you to connect with people on that level.

With his recent book, *Money, Master the Game*, Tony has decided to tread where every man has gone before: into the financial services industry. His book contains some valuable financial advice for those able to get through the forty-five chapters of this book, which is also supplemented with Tony's usual dose of self-help motivation talk. Although off-putting to many, I like reading the "I can be anything" sections of the book.

The problem is that for six hundred pages Tony takes the position of an objective outsider, who has arrived to provide you with the independent, fiduciary advice you need to move your financial life forward. With a phonebook-size guide full of financial self-help and some Warren Buffet quotes, this must have been a publisher's dream!

The conflicts start with his recommendation for an investment firm called Stronghold Wealth Management, which he says isn't like those "other" firms trying to screw you over all the time. According to his book, "they provide complete transparency as the core operating principle."

As of the release of his book, Tony was set to be an owner in Stronghold Wealth Management. His son, a financial advisor in San Diego, was also going to be part of the project. He has been pilloried by the financial media for this potential connection since the book arrived—with many calling it out as a conflict of interest and lack of transparency. Tony backed out of that deal before the book was released and now has no affiliation with Stronghold.

Let's look at what actually happened though: Tony Robbins wrote a book to promote to a new company of his. That new company happens to be a fee-only investment firm, the most ethical and conflict-free way to enter the investment business. Although he did not disclose his plans in the book, he disclosed them in required investment documents. Anyone have a problem with this? It's a little bait-and-switchy but certainly nothing dishonest. Adding value to the consumer by writing an educational book, even to promote a new business, seems reasonable to me.

My issue is later in the book when he discusses indexed annuities and a venture he has partnered in called Lifetime Income. The goal of Lifetime Income is to sell you a product called a fixed index annuity (FIA), which Tony discusses extensively in his book.

The merits of a particular FIA are not the subject of this chapter, but here are the basics: Some FIAs are good, and some are not good. Some are appropriate; some are not appropriate. They are all insurance products that can be sold without an investment license, and the commissions to the various entities selling them can be as high as 10 percent.

When you call the 800 number in Tony's book, your call goes to the largest annuity distributor in the country that then connects you with a member of its sales force to sell you an annuity. More often than not, the salespeople will use a proprietary product that pays them more commission, and Tony is paid out of that on the back end, up to 25 percent of the commission.

Most financial recommendations from anyone—at any time—will have some type of conflict or payment attached to it. Again, this is not dishonesty from Tony Robbins. It is simply a case of someone using his platform to suggest he is here to finally provide independent advice and then give you anything but.

Not how you thought that worked? You probably suspected it did but hoped it did not.

Financial Institutions

Perhaps there is no greater demonstration of motives versus incentives than looking at the large financial institutions in our country. It is hard to picture today, but there was once a time when the great financial institutions of our nation were respected. We relied on these great companies to give us access to investments, help us plan for retirement, and provide insurance for our families. Now, I cannot recall the last time I spoke with a client who did not treat a major investment firm with skepticism.

You already know this, either intuitively or through experience, but let me confirm it for you: major Wall Street firms and banks don't give a shit about you. There may have been a time when they did but not since I have been in the business. These conflict-ridden blights on society that dominate our financial landscape are responsible for producing two things and two things only: products and salespeople.

I have read too many marketing and sales books over the years trying to improve and grow my business, and most of them have a consistent theme: if you are selling products, pretend you are selling advice.

No industry has mastered this concept more than the investment industry. Pay attention to the next commercial you see on TV for a major investment firm. It's all about "trust," "helping you achieve your goals," and "being there for the long-term." The only problem is that everyone single one of these firms is trying to sell you products masquerading as advice.

For a major investment firm, what percentage of their revenue do you think comes from offering advice as opposed to selling products? Products are "what's for dinner," not advice.

Financial *advice* is important because it focuses on *you*. Your needs come first, and the only solutions offered are the ones that improve your financial life. Deciding between products carries the stress of making the right decision for your family, receiving advice reduces stress in your life by solving your problems.

The second output we see from a large firm is salespeople, and here is where most investors get confused. They think that a good advisor at one of these firms can take care of them, even if this advisor works in a corrupt system or firm. The investor is once again staking his or her personal fortune on the motives of the advisor he or she is working with.

I have met many of these advisors, and I would venture to say that nearly all these men and women are good people who do have your best interests in mind. But how do you know their motives are pure, and how would you ever know for sure? You can't, and you won't.

What you can know for sure is what their incentives are, and those incentives are determined by their employer. It doesn't matter how great the advisor is or how pure the motives. If the incentive structure is skewed, your results will be too.

How much are you willing to bet that your big-firm advisor can overcome the odds and work within the system for your benefit? Are you willing to bet 1 percent a year in extra fees? Are you willing to wager a successful thirty-year retirement? How about gambling that your spouse will be well taken care of if you are gone?

Those are very high stakes. Are you sure the horse you want to ride is hope that a giant Wall Street firm will act in your best interests? That seems like a bold move to me and a completely unnecessary one. Why do investors continually choose hidden agendas over an incentive structure they can see, confirm, and understand?

Employees have motives, but the firm determines the incentives—and the firm doesn't care about you.

Incentive Capital Management, LLC

Some financial planning firms charge up front for a financial plan—typically $2,500 to $5,000—and some do not. The ones that don't charge up front will not start your plan until you have moved your investment accounts over to their firm where they are getting paid a management fee. Getting paid for your work seems like a reasonable concept to me; I have no problem with either business model.

The problems with this arrangement started when big insurance companies started having their insurance salespeople masquerade around town as financial planners, and a new business model was born.

Under this new business model, you wrote the insurance company a check for a "financial plan." You answered a bazillion questions, and then a couple of weeks later, you had a meeting with your "planner" where you were presented a huge binder filled with about a hundred pages of recommendations that you will never read, understand, or otherwise reference again in your life.

That is okay though because our helpful planners have summarized their findings into one page of recommendations for you to review. Any guesses what is on there? You got it: you need more insurance! Great. Where do I get that? You are in luck. I have the exact product you need!

Getting paid to tell people to buy more stuff from you? It's a great gig if you can get it. And these plans don't say "buy more insurance" sometimes; they say it *every time.*

Many "independent" firms have followed suit because it is a profitable business model. A firm can charge you up front for a financial plan, then make a huge commission on the insurance products they recommend, and make money on an ongoing basis for managing your investment accounts.

Maybe two out of three times are okay, but there should be a limit. Before you cut anyone a check, be sure to know how else this person will be generating revenue from your nest egg.

Is that Real Italian Leather?

One of the most entertaining things about being in this business is competing against the same competition all the time. It seems like there is an endless number of people who have decided to accept what the big national firms and banks are offering as "advice."

My favorite part comes halfway through the first meeting when the investment statements from their current firm are pulled out of the manila folder. I always love to see what logo is on page one. Once I see the logo, I know exactly what they are invested in without looking. The conversation usually goes something like this:

"I see you are with Edward Jones. Do you know what you are invested in there?"

"Yes, I understand most of it. They put a portfolio together tailored for our specific needs, based on our risk tolerance," they usually reply. "It's a custom portfolio."

"That is great," I explain to them, trying to walk the line between sincere and smug, and probably failing. "Does your 'custom portfolio' include a Lincoln variable annuity, American Funds, and something called a UIT from someplace called Van Kampen?"

"I think so; how did you know…"

Because I am huge smartass; that is how. And I have been doing this for fifteen years. And like most of the people in this country, they are paying an advisor thousands of dollars a year for about two hours of work, including meeting time. Cookie-cutter doesn't begin to describe the portfolios these companies put together.

I gain new clients from large, national firms on a regular basis. I rarely gain new business by transferring clients from a local, independent financial planning firm. The clients of these firms are seldom shopping advisors, and they are typically happy with the service they are receiving.

Remember, it isn't that employees of the big firms don't *want* to do the right thing or aren't *trying* to do the right thing for you. The reality is that they are constantly incentivized to help the firm at the expense of truly independent recommendations.

CHAPTER 3

GOOD BUSINESS MODEL VS. BAD BUSINESS MODEL

I t is my second meeting with a financial planning prospect—a couple—and things are going very well. I have spent a lot of time asking about their goals, what they want to accomplish with their money, and some of the positive and negative experiences they have had in the past with money. Nobody had asked them these questions before. It is important to determine exactly what they value in life and how to make their money work *for* those values.

The list of areas in which I can improve this couple's situation is rapidly expanding. Their portfolio is too risky, no one is managing taxes, they are underinsured, and the fees are a bit ridiculous. They had clearly been sold a series of products with no underlying plan or understanding by anyone how the pieces all fit together.

We agree on all this. It is one of those fortunate situations where my improvements aren't really opinion, as they often are, but based on facts I can use to help them. Yet I am sensing some hesitation to move forward. Like a lot of good people, they are worried about hurting the feelings of the advisor they have been with for five years.

"We really like him though," they explain to me. "We would feel bad moving our accounts."

"I'm sure he is a very nice guy." I enter the conversation carefully. "But I want to recap here: you said you aren't happy with your accounts, you feel lost without a plan, you are pretty sure he doesn't know what he is doing because he can rarely answer your tough questions, and we agree that all the improvements on the table in front of us are items that will help you immediately. They will not help you because I said they would; they will help you because of math and logic. Am I off on any of this?"

"No, everything you are saying makes sense," they say. "It's just that his assistant is so nice to us, he sends us birthday cards, and his firm throws a great Christmas party every year. They have a nice office too."

"Well…" I reply.

Actual Conversation	Conversation in My Head
Me: I understand there is an emotional connection there. Getting in a mind-set of doing what is best for *you* is not always easy.	**Me:** Are you fricking kidding me?
	Them: Excuse me?
Them: I know he is trying his best for us. We just feel like if we leave, it would be disloyal. We would also be down one of our favorite Christmas parties of the year! (Fake laughter all around.)	**Me:** I'm saving you thousands of dollars a year in fees and know what I am doing, and you are unsure what to do?
	Them: But the staff is so nice, and this Christmas party is awesome!
Me: That is a good point, but we are going to try our best for you, and I love to throw a great Christmas party as well. (Half true. I do try my best, but I hate Christmas parties and refuse to have them.)	**Me:** How dense are you? You're paying an extra $5,000 a year in fees for a Christmas party? How about you take that extra money and throw an epic Christmas party for your friends and family. Those are people we just spent two meetings identifying you would like to spend more time and resources on.
Them: We just need to think about it some more.	

Me: I understand what you are saying, but I want to be clear on what you are thinking about. You are not deciding between your old advisor and me. You do not have to decide who is nicer, smarter, and funnier. You are deciding which of us has a *business model* that makes sense to take care of you and your family.	**Them:** Maybe you haven't seen the office. It's downtown *and* has a view of the water. **Me:** I'm going to slap you now. But because I am a gentleman, I am going to bring in one of our female advisors to slap your wife.

And so it goes. Lots of good people refuse to act in their own best interests because of an emotional attachment to a person, place, or idea. We see the same thing in the medical field—patients actively ignoring the advice of a doctor, refusing to take medicine, or plain living in denial that they need medical care. I guess it should not be too surprising that we see the same behavior in finance.

Conflicting Conflicts

As we discussed earlier, conflicts of interest cannot be entirely eliminated in any profession. Instead, we must learn to manage them effectively. Below is a list of common business models that are being used today and the conflicts that are inherent in each of them.

Remember, the existence of conflicts does not mean a particular solution is not the right one for you. Conflicts must simply be identified and evaluated; only then can a decision be made on whether the solution is the right one for you.

- **Financial advisor:** Most advisors still hold licenses that allow them to sell products for a commission. They can get paid an up-front fee if you move money to them.
- **Insurance agent:** Agents are paid more for recommending one product over another. Being loyal to one product will pay them more and give them additional perks.
- **Financial planner:** If they charge hourly or with a fixed fee, they have an incentive to make your financial plan unnecessarily complicated or cut corners.
- **Big bank:** The focus is always on selling products, and good advice will be by coincidence.
- **Wall Street:** Proprietary products dominate this space. Big firms will have kickbacks on their kickbacks and almost always have a reason they are recommending one product over another.
- **Media:** Our financial media grow revenues by increasing the number of readers, listeners, and viewers who follow them. Increasing the size of the audience will always take precedence over giving sound financial advice.
- **Online brokerages:** They want you trading stocks yourself. The conflict here is that they will always tell you that you have enough skill and experience to handle your own finances and that paying any fees to anyone is unreasonable.

- **Coworker/cousin/neighbor:** Friends only give investment advice for one reason: to show you how smart they are. They will not be honest with you about the trouble they have had and the bad stocks they have picked. Their financial advice will be like a Facebook page where you only see a highlight reel of the good stuff that happened.

Conflicts are to be identified, evaluated, and understood—not eliminated.

Education Gap

What most of the business models above have in common is that they have no reason to educate you on how to make an informed decision. Why would eTrade tell you about the value that a good financial advisor can provide? Why would a big bank help you with your retirement income plan when it can pull another sucker out of the teller line to push overpriced products on?

The answer is they wouldn't, and they don't. The incentive to educate the consumer on how the financial world functions so they can make an informed decision does not exist anywhere. How am I going to jam high-commission products down your throat if you know how I benefit from it?

Hopefully, you are picking up a consistent theme by now: pay for advice. I read a sales book recently where it said if you are selling something complicated, make it sound simple, and if you are selling something simple, make it sound complicated. This advice is clearly taken to an extreme in our industry.

The products that should be easy like insurance now have all kinds of unnecessary complications attached to them. The same goes for selecting an investment allocation. Financial planning, however, is very complicated and time consuming, yet most investors feel all planners are doing is plugging their data into an online calculator. We need to do better.

There are resources out there to educate you, and you must keep searching until you find them. The financial industry we have created in this country is not going to help you find truly independent education on how to make smart choices with your money.

It's time to get back to the basics with your finances. Take the time to understand what a good spending and investment plan looks like for *you* and how it will get *you* closer to where you want to be. If you don't take the time to understand what you want your money to do for you in this life, you will own the wrong things.

Stop consuming products. Start consuming advice.

Independent Capital, LLC

I am as guilty as the next guy: I have used the word *independent* in my marketing for as long as I can remember. Truth be told, I still use it to this day. It feels good to use, like it's more of a mission statement than a marketing statement.

When I brag of my independence, it means several different things: owning my own firm, not having a boss, having no sales quotas to meet and no additional compensation for using one product over another, not receiving any kickbacks from vendors, and so on. Basically, to me it means I have no incentive not to act in my clients' best interests at any given time.

Others seem to define that word differently. The problem is that the word *independent* now means so many things in the financial industry that it means nothing. I have seen bank employees call them themselves independent. What? You work for Goliath National Bank where you raise your hand to take a leak. If that's independence, I would hate to see how you define captive.

Words losing their original meaning is hardly rare in society today. Is there any business that can't provide us *value?* This trend is slightly annoying in everyday life, but when it comes to your money, it's terrifying. We are allowed to use random words like *independent, advice,* and *improvement* even when we are offering none of those things.

Don't be scared off by the word independent. The good guys still use that term as well. Just know that casually dropping trustworthy words into marketing materials has become a common strategy, even when those words no longer have meaning.

Sweet Business Model, Bro

How Does The Top Insurance Agents in Our Industry Continue to Make High Six -Figure Income?, The Answer is, They Have 20 to 30 New Annuity Marketing Leads Every Week...Doing What You Aren't!

This is what I see pretty much every single day in my inbox. And yes, typically with typos. Every morning, some marketing nonsense about how I am going to triple my income with very little work. Any guesses what types of people are attracted to fill the lower end of this industry?

Everyone in this business thinks they understand finance, and sadly they think this is the same as understanding financial planning. By now, you know that isn't true.

The most frustrating aspect of being a good advisor is that you are rarely rewarded for being a good advisor. Rewards in this business are reserved primarily for good salespeople. Those who can sell products get paid. Those who focus on providing great advice either learn how to sell, partner with someone who can sell, or wash out of the industry.

The business model for any new person entering this business is to sell you high-commission products that you don't understand. This is the only way for a big firm to pay for the cost of hiring a new salesperson. The part you typically miss is that the person selling doesn't understand the product either. You don't have to settle for financially illiterate salespeople new to the business. There are better options.

There is only one way someone can get experience. I don't begrudge anyone hustling to make a living or starting a business. That is the route I took.

Why would you pay a new guy who is hustling to sell products instead of paying a new gal who is hustling to offer advice?

CHAPTER 4

VICTIM VS. THRIVING

U p to this point, we have established that many financial advisors suck, most large Wall Street firms are indeed out to screw you over, and your "friends" in the media are not providing you with actionable advice on how to find solutions to your problems. It's almost enough to throw your hands in the air, but only after you are done hiding your money in the mattress.

Despite opening this book with three chapters of negativity, the future is not as bleak as it seems. There are thousands of elite financial advisors in this country who specialize in various financial planning disciplines. The problem is they are difficult to find because they suck at marketing.

When looking for an advisor, investors will typically ask friends and family for a referral, search online for information, or attend some type of marketing event. These methods are fine for compiling a list of names to look at, but you can create a list of names by opening the phone book. Finding a *potential* advisor is as easy as finding a potential Realtor: if you stare at a "For Sale" sign too long the Realtor can sense it and will start calling you.

The struggle begins once you have your list even if it is a list of one. There is no method for determining if the advisor has acquired the specialized skill set to solve your specific problems. We get confused about what our problems really are, so it's back to questions about performance and fees.

My all-time favorite "specialty" is from Edward Jones with the "401(k) Rollover Specialists" signs some of their salespeople place in the window of their strip mall stores. It's decent advertising, but do you know what that sign translates to for those of us that are in the business? It means "that sales guy specializes in taking large chunks of your money and making a huge commission from selling you products."

A great specialty indeed. That is like our Realtor friends saying they specialize in selling million-dollar homes for 10 percent over market price without utilizing any marketing strategies. Commissions without good advice is a tremendous business model if you can get it.

There is no perfect checklist for matching you with great financial advice, but we can't give up the search to find the solution that is right for us. For most it will be a search to find the right financial advisor but not for everyone. Some will be fine managing their finances and doing their own financial planning. Not everyone needs to use a financial planner.

Everyone does need good advice, however.

Turning the Corner

Here we go again. I had spent several hours putting together a financial plan for these clients that solved all their problems. They now had an income plan to distribute their investments for retirement that they could count on. My firm also prepared a tax management strategy, life-insurance recommendations, legacy planning, and several other details that would greatly improve their situation.

Despite all the work I had produced, they were receiving advice from about five different sources and were dithering about what to do. Once again, they were unable to differentiate a legitimate provider of advice like myself from others who were selling products. As frustrating as it was, I had only been adding to the problem for several years by doing this work for free up front.

It wasn't until that meeting that I fully understood what a moron I am. What sane person does all the work for free? I do, apparently, along with about half of my colleagues. Without any type of commitment up front, a person will not value what you do.

This deal still had some life in it, however. Even though I didn't take myself seriously enough to charge for my time, they were still getting the message.

"So how do we know this will all work?" they asked me.

"Well..." I replied.

Actual Conversation	Conversation in My Head
Me: You don't know if it will work. We take the best information we have at the time and make the best decisions we can. Every year we will do our best with no guarantees.	**Me:** Are you frickin' kidding me?
	Them: Excuse me?
Them: I know there aren't any guarantees, but this is all the money we have, and we want to make sure that we are making the right decision.	**Me:** How do you know if you will wake up tomorrow? How do you know if your car will start? Just get started on *something*.
Me: I totally understand. This is a lot of money, and it's everything to you. But at some point, you must move forward. Being nervous is not a very good financial plan.	**Them:** But everybody is saying such different things. We just don't know what to do.
	Me: You don't know what to do? Everyone is trying to sell you products everywhere you turn. Most of the recommendations you have received involve huge commissions, and the rest come from some website or neighbor that thinks they have a secret investment strategy.
Them: I know. And you and your staff will be here for us no matter what, through the ups and downs of the market and the ups and downs of our life?	**Them:** Good point—let's move forward with you.

Me: You know I will. It's what I do for my job. **Them:** Okay, let's move forward.	**Me:** Additionally, these stupid...wait, what did you say? Was that a yes? Holy crap, maybe there is hope for the future!

How to Analyze a Financial Advisor Business Model

One way to gather information on what type of financial advisor you are working with is by looking at their business card or website. The term "financial advisor" is very generic and can mean a variety of things. By digging a little deeper, we can learn more about what type of business model they have committed to, and what the ramifications of that decision will mean for your finances.

The title on the business card will often mean something very specific. Knowing what types of investment firms utilize which titles will give you a head start in determining the conflicts you are likely to encounter.

Registered Representative

Typically, you will find a registered representative sitting in the lobby of a bank or credit union. They carry a restricted license where they can only advise on certificate of deposits (CDs), annuities, and mutual funds. And what a coincidence—these recommendations are usually that you purchase mutual funds and CDs that the bank owns!

Corporate tells them exactly which products they can recommend. Their flow of new business comes from the tellers in the branches that are coached to notice you have money in your savings and should talk to the twenty-three-year-old "advisor" sitting in the corner.

In recent years, moving clients from savings accounts to mutual funds and CDs has not been enough for the banks. Now, they will typically recommend you purchase a very expensive—and very unnecessary—variable annuity that the bank will receive a huge commission on. The bank can make as much as 8 percent in commission by selling you this product.

Insurance Agent

Even if the card says financial advisor instead of insurance agent, you are still looking for the insurance company logo to see if the person works for a large insurance company. These insurance companies are still a popular entry point into the business for many because commissions can be generated quickly by selling insurance policies to friends and family.

After a salesperson is hired, they secure life/disability insurance licenses, which usually include the ability to sell annuities as well. The process of helping people make decisions on life and disability insurance involves talking about money, future objectives, and fears. It sort of looks and feels like financial planning to the consumer.

However, the license is to sell insurance products, not to provide financial advice. They can't talk about investments, so they usually partner with someone who can. The insurance company pays them a commission when they sell an insurance or annuity product.

Stock Brokers

These almost need no explanation because movies have painted a vivid stereotype for us. From *Wall Street* to *Boiler Room* and many other great movies, stock brokers yelling "buy" and "sell" is what many investors think of when investing comes to mind.

If you were having trouble understanding the difference between someone who sells advice and one who is selling products, hopefully this clears up the confusion. A stock broker is trying to sell you whatever he or she can with little regard to your personal financial situation.

Selling securities for a commission requires a broker to pass a test called the Series 7, which encompasses the trading of stocks, corporate bonds, municipal bonds, treasuries, mutual funds, and options. It is very important to understand that stock broker types *are not legally required to make a recommendation that's in your best interest—ever.* They only have to justify that the investment may be "suitable" for you.

Some consumers like the idea of their broker calling them with hot stock tips—even if those so-called tips are really just moving the firm's security of the month. They only get paid when they buy or sell positions for your portfolio—which explains why there is always a better investment next month you should be looking at.

Media Experts

We hit this one hard earlier, but it's worth revisiting. Media personalities have no idea what's going on with *your* financial life. Their "advice" appears free, but is the most expensive on the market. It's laced with conflict of interest like you've never seen before.

They answer to bosses, publishers, advertisers, and product sponsors. They do not answer to regulators, and the most popular personalities are never licensed to give investment advice nor have they ever been. You read that right. They fly under the radar using a loophole for the media so they don't have to be educated, licensed, or held accountable.

Financial Planners

As you may have noticed, the major takeaway from this book is to pay for advice by hiring a professional advice giver—pardon the technical language there. Someone who is selling you products is not a good place to get advice. There is no better place to start your search to receive advice then with a financial planner.

Similar to attorneys, financial planners must act as impartial fiduciaries in order to charge for their advice. They produce written plans that address accumulation goals, expenses, debt, cash flow projections, investments, insurance, and taxes. They make a living charging for the advice they give. Most financial planners will not manage your assets until they have done real financial planning for you.

Unfortunately, there is no license that corresponds with being a financial planner. There is nothing stopping you from printing business cards that say "Financial Planner" on them and giving financial advice tomorrow. For real. You can't advise on specific investments strategies, but you could give financial advice on every other topic without being licensed.

Although there is still not a license that corresponds with financial planning, there is a certification and it's legit. I know it is legit because I have it, and the test sucks to take. A certified financial planner® (CFP®) is someone who has put in the work to understand all aspects of building a personal financial plan.

According the CFP Board, a CFP® must master nearly one hundred integrated financial planning topics, including

- investment planning,
- tax planning,
- retirement planning,
- estate planning,
- risk management,
- insurance planning, and
- financial management.

Other requirements include passing a comprehensive six-hour examination, a minimum of three years of experience, and agreeing to abide by a strict code of professional conduct known as CFP Board's "Code of Ethics and Professional Responsibility."

A CFP® designation is not a guarantee of success or competency for an advisor. They can be just as big of turds as other advisors. You must start somewhere, however, and your odds of finding the right advice will increase greatly by associating with a CFP®.

Credentials are not created equal. Understand what a CFP® can do.

How to Analyze Investment Performance

Don't. Seriously, don't do it. Advisors can make an outhouse look like a mansion—you need to trust me on this. We are trained to make a perfectly adequate portfolio that a competitor puts together look like complete garbage. Don't believe me? Take a look at this analysis I prepared, these numbers are all accurate as of the writing of this book:

> *Investment A*—I looked at one of the holdings in your current portfolio, and quite frankly, it is far too risky for what you are trying to accomplish. Just since I have been in this business, this investment you are holding has cratered in value over 50 percent *twice.* I can't imagine recommending something to my clients that would be cut in half on two separate occasions! Over the last ten years, it has returned a respectable 6 percent on average, but taking on the risk of losing half your money in order to make 6 percent doesn't make sense to me. I have an insurance product that can't go backward and should make you 6 percent *tax-free.* Let's look at repositioning some of these assets to more closely align with your risk tolerance.

> *Investment B*—I have a great investment opportunity for you to look at. It has averaged over 15 percent per year for the last five years and produces a 2 percent dividend along with it. Looking back, it has not had a negative year in almost ten years, and not again until five years before that. The outlook moving forward is very positive as well; I expect double-digit growth to continue for the next several years.

Did you see it? Both investments are the S&P 500, but I made one of them sound riskier than back-alley surgery and the other seem almost too good to be true. This is just the tip of the iceberg when it comes to presenting investments. Once we involve multiple-asset classes, multiple money managers, hypothetical data (i.e., bullshit data), and cherry-picked time frames, we are basically making things up to show you.

Most *advisors* can't distinguish one good investment strategy from another. Spending your time trying to analyze if the details of a particular approach makes sense for you is madness—it will never work. Understanding the *incentives* behind the recommendation is the only plan that will get you closer to your goals.

If you keep asking about performance, your advisor will keep making shit up.

How to Analyze Fees

We can get into all the ways a financial advisor and Wall Street firms can take money out of your pocket and put it into their own, but I want to keep this book under one thousand pages. There are nearly unlimited combinations of business models, fee structures, and kickback arrangements that make it difficult to determine exactly what is going on inside your account.

That does not mean you are powerless, however. The easiest way to get a sense of what you are paying to who is simple: just ask. Ask your advisor this one simple question: for every dollar I invest with you, list out the parties that are getting paid on that dollar and approximately how much.

If you ask this simple question, you will discover one of two things: (1) You will find out what your fees are, or (2) you will know it's time to start looking for a new advisor.

Chances are excellent they either won't know all the parties getting paid or will casually leave a few out. You would be amazed how advisors can convince themselves that their firm isn't taking more money out of your account behind the scenes.

Knowledge on fees begins by asking. Once you have an answer—any answer—you can start to research to see if your advisor is telling the truth or not. Call me a skeptic, but my guess is that over 75 percent of you are not going to get the straight answer.

How to Analyze Your Behavior

Study after study after study shows that the biggest driver of investment returns is the behavior of the investors themselves. We are hardwired to buy high, sell low, and constantly be on the lookout for the next great investment. We always have this feeling that our neighbor has something better, and we need to be on the lookout for it so we don't miss out.

Clients and prospects are continuously asking about what they think might be the next great solution. The number of questions I get about investing in gold always take me aback. I used to be nuanced in my answer, but now I just tell people my opinion: that is a really stupid idea. Don't do it.

And if it isn't gold, it's something else. Somebody found a newsletter online, and this person says the market is going to crash, and they correctly predicted the last one so you should listen. What evidence is provided to back up the claims? It basically boils down to *because I said so.* If it's on the Internet, it must be true.

We are all susceptible to sales pitches, and we all want to believe somebody has a great idea we just stumbled upon. That part of the process will never change; the part that matters is what comes next. What will we do with that information, how will we *behave.*

The best way to control what is the largest variable—your behavior—in the investment equation is to find somebody who can help you make the right decisions at the right time and avoid the wrong ones. This is accomplished by finding an advisor whose advice you trust and respect. The road map for finding an advisor remains the same as it was at the beginning of this book: pay for advice, not products.

You don't need an advisor—as long as you can see your blind spots.

Magic Investments, LLC

I have been the chief compliance officer of investment firms for half of my career. Rules and regulations are not foreign to me, but I am still amazed that certain firms have not been sued into submission.

I ran across one particularly egregious firm a couple of years ago. The key to its success must have been everyone working until the sun came up because no one there could possibly be sleeping at night with what they were doing. Also, mirrors were probably removed from the bathrooms to avoid self-reflection.

Let's start with the fees. An investment advisor on the high end of the fee structure will charge around 1.5 percent annually, with larger accounts often at 1 percent. This firm was charging 2.75 percent just for the privilege of using their strategies. We can add mutual-fund costs to that list as well, putting the strategy well over 3.5 percent.

What investment strategy was so good that it was worth paying triple the going rate? This strategy had produced annual returns of 13 percent over the last ten years with no down years. You read that right—no down years to go along with great upside. Maybe this idea is worth 3.5 percent.

Except this strategy, like all magic investment strategies, was not real. The manager this firm was using had "back-tested" investment performance. For the uninitiated, this means that for the period the return numbers are being shown, this strategy did not exist, and nobody was invested in this strategy. This is all perfectly legal.

Where it gets shady is when you imply that these numbers are real. Genuine investment strategies will have an audit—a specific type of audit—to prove that the numbers are real. This firm did not conduct this type of audit; instead, it hired a small CPA firm to audit the fake numbers and verify that all the fake numbers were added up correctly! This left the impression that the numbers were real, when they are far from it.

Because experienced advisors know how this game is played, this firm recruited new advisors who did not know any better. They were told to ask their clients how they would like to make 13 percent per year *after fees* with no downside, and these poor investors jumped at the chance. This firm grew to over a billion dollars using this technique.

When the actual return numbers started coming in, these investors lagged the market by about 70 percent.

It is infuriating to watch these firms build a business based on BS. It is satisfying to watch them crumble under the weight of their deception. But mostly, it is sad that so many investors work their tails off to accumulate assets and then hand them over to these incompetent assholes.

The Magic Investment Strategy

The client leaned back in his chair, crossed his arms, and said, "Okay, let me ask you this." Oh boy, I have seen this one before. *Nobody* sells this guy. He is here to ask me the tough questions! At least he thinks they are tough questions. "What has your performance been?"

What this really signals is he has no idea what he is talking about.

"Eight," I reply.

"What do you mean eight?" he asks. "Over what time frame, and what is your strategy?"

"For what time frame and for what type of strategy were you asking about?" I say. "Because maybe it isn't eight. Maybe it is actually seven or nine."

He has no idea I am messing with him. I have hundreds of clients with hundreds of different goals who started with my firm at hundreds of different points in time. Return numbers are everywhere. Even if I had those numbers, I wouldn't share them. The market determines your returns, not me.

"What would you consider good performance?" I ask him.

"Well, beating the market would be good performance for starters," he said.

"Okay, I think my number eight beats the market, so we are good there," I tell him.

"Okay, if you say so," he replies, as if there are any facts in this conversation. "But the last guy I met with had this strategy that has returned 13 percent per year over the last ten years, with no down years. That seems pretty good to me."

"That does seem pretty good, especially if he had a glossy marketing sheet that said 13 percent on it. But I have a question for you. If someone owned a strategy that could return 13 percent with no downside, why in the hell would you ever be offered an opportunity to invest in it?"

"Excuse me?"

"Think about it. If that strategy really existed, the only certainty is that you would never have access to it with your $250,000 and neither would I. Even if I invested all my clients in it, it would be small potatoes. If there was a strategy that could do that in the real world, some Wall Street firm or hedge fund would have paid a trillion dollars for it already."

"But the guy said…"

"People say a lot of things. There has only been one manager to produce double-digit returns, on a consistent basis, with no down years, to his clients over an extended period of time. His name was Bernie Madoff, and he ran the biggest Ponzi scheme in history."

"I guess it does seem a little unlikely," he admitted.

"A little unlikely? Why would this scrub who is two years into being an 'advisor' have access to the greatest investment strategy of all time?"

I'm running out of ways to say it: go find a good financial planner, and then go live your life. There are only two possibilities when it comes to the magic investment strategy: (1) it doesn't exist, or (2) it already exists, and you will never have access to it as long as you live because it was classified "Top Secret" immediately after it was created.

CHAPTER 5

CONCLUSION

**Holy shit, they all look the same to me
—Everybody not in this business**

Tom and Mary were exhausted. They had spent the better part of three months meeting with financial advisors and conducting research online. The more time they put in, the more confusing the options became. The more they narrowed down their options, the less certain they became that they were making the right choice.

They were friends of friends, and so when I was introduced, my goal was not to make them clients. They had enough options for advisors to work with but just didn't understand exactly what they would be paying for. My offer was to help them sort through all the data that had been gathered to date so they could make a wise decision.

The first advisor they met with told them they were taking on too much risk. He explained that most of their money was in the stock market and we would be experiencing a correction soon. When that correction comes, they could lose as much as half of what they had accumulated. Did they want to lose half of their money? Of course not, Tom told me.

The solution that was recommended by the first advisor was to move the majority of the money into an insurance product that could not go backward but could still make money if the market went up. I asked them how much he was recommending they invest. Mary told me of the $800,000 they had in investable assets, he thought $600,000 was a good number to keep safe. Did they understand how that product worked? No, Tom said, but they liked the idea of keeping their money safe.

It makes sense. Everyone wants to keep his or her money safe. But then I explained that they would be locking their money up for ten years into a product they do not understand and paying the dude they are talking to $40,000 to $50,000 in commissions for the privilege. *This is a product pitch, not financial advice.* Next.

Tom and Mary weren't getting a great feeling from the one-man show they had just met with anyway and were not surprised by my comments. Their next step was to try something drastically different from the first person and meet with a large investment firm downtown that was connected to a bank.

Mary told me she felt a lot more comfortable meeting with the large firm, even if parking downtown did suck. She liked that it was established, had been giving advice for decades, had many advisors in the office, and as a national bank had capabilities that local firms in the area did not. This certainly seemed like the safe route to them.

I don't know that I would call it safe, I explained to them, but it is certainly the most predictable. I knew exactly what the bank was going to recommend to them without even knowing who they would meet with there. Their portfolio would look identical to thousands of other investors', and I know what insurance products would be sold at review meetings to generate additional revenue for the bank.

Their instincts were right that they would probably not get screwed over at the bank, but they needed to prepare for a portfolio of C+ products for the rest of their life. Almost all recommendations they would receive from the bank would include proprietary products or those that have revenue sharing (kickbacks) on the back end. Who do you think pays for those offices? I explained to them that the "free" financial planning advice they would receive from the bank certainly wasn't paying for the many leather-bound books and rich mahogany in the office. They were paying one way or another.

That made sense to Tom. He agreed they were a little squirrelly when he asked about the various methods the firm would be compensated. Quite simply, I informed them, you would be paying a premium for a national brand name. Why someone would pay a higher fee for a limited lineup of investment solutions is beyond me, I told them, but that was just my opinion.

The next advisor Tom and Mary met with was very intriguing, they told me. She had access to an investment strategy that few other advisors in town did. This strategy could basically capture most of the gains in the market while avoiding nearly all the downside. Tom said they looked at the performance of the fund going back to 2000, and it had beat the market by a huge margin. Getting growth in their portfolio and not worrying about losing sounded great to Mary; they were planning on meeting with this nice lady again.

I had one question for them: if this strategy really did that, wouldn't the bank they met with earlier—or some competitor—have already bought it for a billion dollars? If there really is a strategy that can consistently beat the market, why would some random advisor have access to it but not a firm with billions of dollars of assets under management? Good question, they admitted.

The answer is because those returns are bullshit. I can find a hundred of those managers right now and offer their strategies to you. Nearly all of them have back-tested (i.e., made up) return numbers, and you are buying nothing more than the ability of a firm to put pretend numbers on a glossy brochure that looks good. Tell me the number that was on the brochure, and I will find you a strategy I have access to that beats it in two minutes.

They did—and then I did. I was able to find a few strategies that told a very good story and had a "return" higher than the one they had just seen. The investment performance game is a tempting one but must be avoided at all costs. If you are selling investment performance, it means the cupboard is probably bare for real value that you can provide to a client.

Performance is in the past, and that is a small part of the future.

A Financial Plan

The last person Tom and Mary met with was much different than the previous ones. She wanted them to have a financial plan. The plan, she said, would determine what their investment portfolio would look like and if they needed insurance products. They remembered bits and pieces of things she had said to them:

- I can't make a recommendation because I don't know you yet.
- There is not a secret investment strategy; *you* will be the biggest factor in what your returns are.
- Low fees are important, but receiving value for your fees is far more important.

Although we were clearly talking about a fiduciary advisor who wants to act in the client's best interest, Tom and Mary still couldn't see the difference. They weren't sold on the last advisor because they were unable to compare the products she would offer and the recommendations she would make with those of the other advisors. She had provided them with far less detail, and so they were uncomfortable moving forward.

Tom and Mary were unable to recognize the solution that was best for them because the financial services industry has trained them to look for the wrong things. Instead of deciding who is most likely to provide the advice they desperately need, it was the advisors' product sales pitch that stood out from each meeting.

I patiently explained to Tom and Mary that they were attempting to determine what the best financial strategies and products were—*they were trying to analyze the investments themselves.* If they were capable of this, why did they need an advisor at all? Why not just do it themselves? Because they didn't fully understand the products, they told me.

And we are back into the endless feedback loop. Tom and Mary were trying to pick the "best" solution in an area they did not have expertise and were not likely to acquire the necessary expertise. As an experienced advisor, I can very clearly see which path is best for them, even though they could not.

Again, it's not their fault. The pressure on investors to understand the mechanics of financial strategies is enormous. Tom and Mary felt like most of their friends and family did. They thought, "Everyone else seems to get this stuff and are having success. I just need to keep looking." It's not their fault, and it's not your fault you don't know what to do.

The Next Steps

If you want to get serious about your finances and ensure you are making the best decisions possible for the future, you have two options.

The first option is to learn how to manage your own finances. The foundation of this option would be to understand the basics of budgeting and investing, but it would also need to include retirement, tax, insurance, estate, and education planning.

Acquiring the knowledge and experience necessary to give yourself competent financial advice is doable. It just takes time and effort. It takes about four or five years of solving client problems in this business before you have a clue what you are doing. Learning enough to be dangerous will take time, but if you are committed, you can do it.

Financial planning is not a matter of intelligence; it is a function of financial knowledge and discipline.

The second option, another wildcard in this scenario, is your behavior. Study after study shows that the biggest factor of your long-term financial success is not what stocks you pick or which budgeting system you pretend to use but rather your financial behavior. Can you continue to make rational decisions regarding your money even when times are tough? Keeping your debt under control and leaving your money in the market during turbulent times is a difficult thing for everyone.

Staying disciplined is not easy. I get it. The kitchen needs to be remodeled, the car just crossed one hundred thousand miles, and flights to Hawaii are pretty cheap right now. The temptations to lose focus on what you want to accomplish are endless. This stuff is hard.

And it's hard for everyone. If you can successfully be your own financial planner despite all the distractions, good for you. If you can't, won't, or are otherwise unwilling, you do have another option. Instead of learning how to become a financial planner or investment genius, you can learn how to *find* the right financial planner.

Either learn how to become a financial planner, or learn how to find to find one.

Understanding the various business models will take time, but it is much more achievable than learning the nine hundred pages in my financial planning handbook. As we discussed earlier, the key is to look at everything through a lens of motives versus incentives.

You will never be able to determine motives—not until we can remotely read minds. Incentives, on the other hand, are something we can figure out. How is this advisor paid? Who does he work for? What are the scenarios where he makes more money from this relationship?

After you determine what those incentives are, ask yourself a question: are you okay with that? If your advisor is any good, he or she deserves to get paid, but are you paying for the right things? Are you receiving financial advice for the fee you are paying rather than paying for someone to sell you this person's own product?

If this all sounds a little daunting, good. As a country, we have dug ourselves a gigantic hole with regards to financial education, and it is time to start crawling out of it. The first step is not reading articles about how your 401(k) fees are too high or how you suck at budgeting. Those things are probably true but are symptoms of the larger illness.

The larger problem is that our regulatory structure is extremely messed up, and consumers have given up on trying to figure who is likely to act in their best interests and who is not. They resort to who "seems like a good guy" and check it off their list. This behavior makes sense to me. It is exactly what I would do too.

Most everyone is a good guy or gal, but this is your life. Dig deeper.

As someone who has now interacted with thousands of advisors through various industry conferences I have attended, investment firms I have worked at, and projects I have done in this industry, I am begging you to learn the differences between these advisors.

At an industry event, it is not uncommon that I would have an advisor on my left who is asking questions about the tax efficiency, risk profile, and expense ratio of the product we are learning about. On my right, the advisor is asking about the commission it pays.

As I speak with each of them during breaks, they fit neatly into the stereotypes I have grown accustomed to in this business. The advisor on my left focuses on financial planning, has training and credentials, and is truly independent. The advisor on my right works for a large firm and is clearly a salesman first. He couldn't care less how the product fits into a financial plan; he is only wondering how much of it he can sell.

And all I can do is sit there and think, "Holy shit. My mom would think these people do the exact same thing."

SUMMARY

For more information on how to find financial advice that doesn't suck, please visit me at www.stlarsen.com for educational videos, checklists, and general guidance on how to navigate the financial services industry to find the advice you need.

- Everyone is incentivized to sell you, not educate you.
- Great advice is an opinion. Conflicts of interest are a fact.
- We are stuck in this unvirtuous cycle of substituting product information for advice.
- We are not missing great advice and great solutions for the consumer; we are missing a road map for the consumer to find them.
- Joe Retirement was busy asking about fees and performance when he should have been asking, "Are you legally obligated to act in my best interest?"
- The great mistake made by consumers is trying to analyze the *motives* of the person who is selling the product instead of his or her *incentives*.
- Pay for advice directly, you cheap bastard.
- Employees have motives, but the firm determines the incentives—and the firm doesn't care about you.
- Conflicts are to be identified, evaluated, and understood—not eliminated.
- Stop consuming products. Start consuming advice.
- Why would you pay a new guy who is hustling to sell products instead of paying a new gal who is hustling to offer advice?

- Credentials are not created equal. Understand what a CFP® can do.
- If you keep asking about performance, your advisor will keep making shit up.
- You don't need an advisor—as long as you can see your blind spots.
- Financial planning is not a matter of intelligence; it is a function of financial knowledge and discipline.
- Either learn how to become a financial planner, or learn how to find to find one.

NEXT STEP

Nobody should have to wonder if their advisor is acting in their best interests. The financial services industry is confusing, and it is always to easier to accept the status quo than to take control for yourself.

You don't need to tackle all your financial problems at once; you simply need to take the next step towards implementing a worry-free plan for managing your finances.

I understand how it feels to be overwhelmed by money. Not only do I see the struggle every day with my clients, but I also have a spouse, kids, mortgage, and a never-ending list of to-dos just like everyone else. To deal with the daily grind, I have people in my corner who help me navigate the struggles of managing personal finances, and I want to make sure you have the resources you need as well.

To take the next step towards creating a simple personal financial plan, download my Worry-Free Money Roadmap at www.stlarsen.com/roadmap.

If you are looking for honesty, transparency, simplicity, and the tools you need to take control of your finances then take the next step towards creating a worry-free money system you can implement immediately by getting my Worry-Free Money Roadmap for free at: www.stlarsen.com/roadmap.

ABOUT THE AUTHOR

Steve Larsen, CPA, CFP®, holds a master of accountancy from Gonzaga University and has over fifteen years of experience as an investment advisor and financial planner. He has also served as an arbitrator for the Financial Industry Regulatory Authority. He lives in the Pacific Northwest with wife and three children.

NOTES

NOTES

NOTES

NOTES

NOTES

NOTES

NOTES

NOTES

NOTES

NOTES

Made in the USA
Lexington, KY
08 February 2018